PEACH M
(MELBA'S LAST FAREWELL)

by

Thérèse Radic

Current Theatre Series
published by Currency Press, Sydney
in association with Playbox Theatre Company, Melbourne

CURRENT THEATRE SERIES

First published in 1990 by
Currency Press Pty. Ltd.,
P.O. Box 452 Paddington, N.S.W. 2021.
Australia, in association with
Playbox Theatre Company, Melbourne

National Library of Australia
Cataloguing-in-Publication data
Radic, Thérèse, 1935-
    Peach Melba : Melba's Last Farewell

    ISBN 0 86819 262 7

    1. Melba, Dame Nellie, 1861-1931 - Drama.
    2. Women singers - Australia - Drama.
    I. Playbox Theatre (Melbourne, Vic.)
    II. Title.
    (Series : Current theatre series).

A822.3

Typeset by Allette Systems P/L, Sydney.
Printed by Bridge Printery, Sydney.

Currency's creative writing program is assisted by the Australia
Council, the Federal Government's arts funding and advisory body.

INTRODUCTION

Who *was* Nellie Melba? According to Max Harris in *The Unknown Great Australians and Other Psychobiographical Portraits* she was: 'the all-Australian world champion bitch...demanding, dictatorial, ruthless, appallingly snobbish, imperious, vain, capricious, inconsiderate, childish, tight- fisted, stingy, mean, ungrateful, pathologically jealous, publicity-hungry and supremely egotistical.'

Percy Grainger thought her: 'rough and intender'(sic) (in *Melodies and Memories*).

The editor of *Truth*, John Norton, accused her publicly of being a drunkard. Baritone Peter Dawson believed she was a gum- chewing, foul-mouthed autocrat (in *Fifty Years of Song*).

Yet this was the woman one of her biographers, Joseph Wechsberg, (in *Red Plush and Black Velvet*), says had everything:

> Commanding presence and beautiful voice, talent and technique, wealth and power. The moment she came on the stage, even before she sang a tone, she could cast a spell. There would be that subtle quickening of her audience's pulse. She was worshipped even by people who had never heard her. She lived at a time that adored its prima donnas and she was the symbol of that time; the best known woman in the world, the most applauded and the most highly paid.

Melba died in Sydney in 1931 from septicemia, the result of an unsuccessful face lift done in Europe some time before. She was nearly seventy. Vanity or bravado? Desperation or courage? Weeping thousands lined the funeral route from Scots' Church in Melbourne to Lilydale cemetery — a three hour drive. State Parliament rose so that members could honour her by standing on the steps of the building as the hearse passed by. And this for the woman Harris describes?

There are a multitude of Melbas, not all of them as ugly as the Dawson or Harris models, or as ideal as Wechsberg's. Paul Sherman's play gives us a dignified matron. Jack Hibberd's version is an endearing larrikin who doesn't know when to keep her mouth shut and who is still doing a comedy routine on her deathbed. The 1950s film turned her into a sexpot. The television series, all gilt and red plush, would have us believe she was the ever gracious lady, incapable of anything as ungenteel as swearing or as necessary as clawing her way to the top. If it is anything to go by Melba is well on her way to becoming a plaster saint. Rather a change from the popular image of 'our Nellie' as a great singer, admirably rich, but fat, coarse, ruthless, bullying and, sin of sins, old.

It wasn't always like that. The Melba of the 1890s had an hour- glass figure, a decent if not distinguished profile, a voice universally admired, an acting ability approved by the critics and a fee of £200 per performance, according to the Covent Garden receipts. In 1892 she sang thirty three times at the Garden — more than any other year, a take of £6,600. The real money was made from singing at high society parties and investing the proceeds under personal instruction from Alfred de Rothschild. Appearances in opera acted as a bait to lure rich matrons into competitive offers for her services.

Her income was dependent on the approval of her patrons — British royalty. As long as the Prince and Princess of Wales turned out for her she was safe. The rest of society followed their lead. Melba could not risk offending them. She made that mistake only once, when her affair with the Duc d'Orleans, heir to the pretender to the French throne, became public knowledge. Her husband, Charles Armstrong, sued for divorce, naming the Duc as co-respondent. The Royals on either side of the channel were not amused. An expected invitation for Melba to sing at Windsor Castle before the Queen failed to materialise. Melba had to decide whether to continue with the Duc or give up her career. She chose her career, ended the affair and never looked back. The accusations of snobbery have less to do with social climbing than career structuring. It was a fact of life that she needed private engagements and buttering up her clients was simply sound business.

The Australian press didn't understand this. Melba was repeatedly rebuked for cultivating high society names, for abandoning her country and, at the end, for having lost what looks she had, put on weight and taken her time about quitting the stage. 'More farewells than Nellie Melba' is now a faded gem of Australese, but it was once a genuinely barbed insult.

Melba was sensitive to all of these accusations but she had a policy of never answering back. Experience had taught her it only added fuel to some gleeful reporters' fire. She needed and sought publicity, as all performers must, but she drew a line at getting it that way. She could have pointed out that the Australian population was too small to support any soloist's career in any case, let alone an opera company. Australia could not afford her, as it could not afford Grainger, Kruse, Hutchinson, Sherwin and dozens of others. Until very recent times the brain drain has always included the best of our artists. To counteract the resentment she knew existed at home Melba returned in 1902 to give concerts in the major cities and to test the water. Would she be welcomed? The reception she got was like a royal progress. In 1909 she came back to let the backblocks farmers hear her. In 1911, 1924 and 1928 she formed opera companies with J. C. Williamson's with the express purpose of offering international performance standards to Australians for the first time, with the ultimate aim of establishing a national company. The accusation that she had abandoned Australia or exploited it when her career was failing is groundless. At no time did her career income falter. Her assertiveness, interpreted by John Norton and others as arrogance, assured that. There is also her own testimony from the memoirs: 'If you wish to understand me at all you must understand first and foremost that I am an Australian.'

It is true that at forty she began to put on weight and that at sixty her waist had disappeared, but if you stand beside her later costumes, so often displayed by the Performing Arts Museum in the foyers of the Victorian Arts Centre, it becomes obvious that she was no more than middle height and, at most, a size sixteen. On stage she appeared taller and bigger. Not quite what Australians expected in the role of the child-bride Juliette or the girlish Mimi, but no more untoward than Sutherland as the daughter of the Regiment and certainly within the tradition of the great opera houses of the day.

The long chain of farewell appearances are another matter. It was the custom for centuries for great performers to raise their retirement funds by giving farewells in the cities that had supported their careers. The greater the musician's fame the more cities there were to milk. The record for such tours was set by Adelina Patti, not Melba. Patti may have needed the money; Melba did not. What she neeed was to be heard by a new generation. She wanted to be remembered, especially by her countrymen. She had lent her considerable reputation to the infant recording industry as early as 1904, but she was never happy with what the primitive technology did to her voice. She recorded close to two hundred items but not one does her justice. The only way for her to counteract that failure was to go on for as long as the voice lasted, which it did to the end, singing before new audiences who could only experience the still intact middle register of her late voice, but who never forgot the magic of her stage presence.

The accusations of meanness and drunkenness are Norton muck flung after Melba left Australia in 1902. Norton's open letter in *Truth* was like shooting someone in the back. He knew Melba could not risk losing a Covent Garden season in order to return to Australia for a defamation case. That would have allowed a rival the chance to step into her shoes. He also knew her reputation for silence in the face of scandal. Norton's own reputation for taking the scythe to tall poppies must have been known to her. She probably thought the whole thing would blow over. No one seemed to care much about his frothing at the mouth over money or sex, but the public took the allegation of drunkeness seriously. On return tours booking offices got used to answering the question: 'Is she sober enough to sing tonight?'

The idea that a top flight coloratura could drink and still maintain a pre-eminent position in the highly competitive world of opera year after year is ludicrous. It is also well nigh impossible because of the physical effects, long term as well as short term, on breathing control and contraction of the throat.

Meanness was hardly one of Melba's vices either. She was deluged with begging letters everywhere she went. Her secretary did a daily weeding out of those under the delusion that Melba was a soft touch and a special account existed to cope with the rest.

What sparked Norton's fire was a good-natured, if somewhat thoughtless gesture on Melba's part during the 1902 tour. There was a drought on. She became concerned at the plight of small farmers in her home state and in an attempt to rouse Melburnians she offered £200 to seed a drought-relief fund. Then she announced that she had also appealed to 'a few of my friends in England and America, who happen to be blest with wealth and influence'. The Council of the Melbourne Chamber of Commerce met in a flurry and issued a statement of disapproval. They argued that Melba was suggesting outside intervention that could damage Australian credit. What had been a goodwill gesture looked as if it could end with Australian stocks falling on the international market simply because the great diva had inadvertently cast doubts on the strength of the economy. The Prime Minister, Edmund Barton, stated in the House that he accepted the views of the Chamber. The Victorian Parliament discussed Melba's motives at some length. Suspicion obliged her to withdraw her offer, but the public, expecting her to stand her ground and carry through her defence of the under-dog, was disappointed, Within days she left for New Zealand. Which is when Norton struck.

In her own day there was a good deal of innuendo published about Melba's sex life but nothing direct was ever said. She was photographed with many men whose names wound up in the gossip columns; but apart from the Duc, she publically admitted to none of them. Minders came came and lovers may have left, but no one ever betrayed Melba's trust. Whatever went on, and certainly a good deal did, it was done with admirable discretion. Today we shrug and say it was her own business, but in an age when merely being a divorcee was suspect (Melba was finally divorced in Texas in 1900), and life upon the wicked stage was presumed to be a very free life indeed, Melba's ability to keep her private life private is remarkable.

There is little doubt that she was a difficult woman, a downright, forthright, outspoken woman capable of using truckers' English when the need arose. She was not inclined to tolerate fools, inefficiency or unprofessional conduct. She drove a hard bargain with theatre managers. She would have been a fool to accept less than she was worth and she knew, as everyone knew, that she was worth more than any other voice of the times, including Caruso's. It is said she used underhand tactics to keep her rivals out of Covent Garden but there is little evidence for this except from the rivals themselves. Suspect evidence, surely. But that she did her damnedest to outsing and outbargain them cannot be denied.

Maybe all the vituperation was plain envy. Maybe it was that famous Australian disease, misogyny. Maybe it is time to realise what Melba was to the women of her day, and certainly is now — a bloody strong-minded woman who knew how to take a superb gift of nature and use it for financial and artistic gain for herself, yes, but also to put her country on the cultural map.

That's a claim not in dispute. On 13 of October 1924 Melba gave her Melbourne farewell. The then Prime

Minister, Stanley Melbourne Bruce, made the curtain speech. Next day the *Age* reported:

> The Prime Minister said he had been set a task that was quite impossible for him to carry out. He had been asked to render to Dame Nellie Melba, on behalf of the people of Australia, their trubute, and make her understand how Australian people regarded her. No man could accomplish that, because there were no words with which to say it. The people of Australia had for her an admiration and esteem which surpassed anything she could conceive. Tonight, at the summit of her wonderful career, they wished to render her tribute. They did so with all the greater feeling because on this night she had done something which was emblematical of the whole of her career. She had associated with her in her triumph the maimed soldiers of Australia. What she had done for Australia no man could say, nor possibly realise. Before the days of the war, and before the Australian soliers had blazoned the name of Australia through the world, Dame Nellie Melba was the ambassador of Australia, and it was she who brought the name of Australia before the nations of the world. The thing which had endeared her most to Australians had been her intense patriotism. She was an inspiration and example to all. She went out in a blaze of glory, and to her retirement would take the good wishes of the whole of the world.

Mr Bruce then kissed Dame Nellie Melba's hand.

Thérèse Radic
April, 1990

Thérèse Radic's biography *Melba: The Voice of Australia* was published by Macmillan in 1986. *Peach Melba* is based on research done for the book.

CHRONOLOGY

1861   Born 19 May as Helen Porter Mitchell daughter of Isabella Ann Dow and David Mitchell, a wealthy builder, at *Doonside*, Richmond, Melbourne.

1875   Attends Presbyterian Ladies College, East Melbourne. Taught Piano by Alice Charbonnet-Kellermann, singing by Mary Ellen Christian (a pupil of Manuel Garcia the Younger, and a London oratorio contralto soloist, who later became a Sister of Charity and founder of the Garcia School of Music, Sydney) and organ by Joseph Summers (a disciple of Mendelssohn, government inspector of music, organist and conductor of the Melbourne Philhamonic Society and organist of the Metropolitan Liedertafel) and Otto Vogt, organist of St Mark's Fitzroy.

1880   Nellie leaves school but continues studies with Pietro Cecchi (Italian tenor formerly with the Lyster Opera Company). Concert career as an amateur continues.

1881   Mother dies in October. Nellie and sister Annie take over housekeeping for family.

1882   In January Nellie's youngest sister Vere, then four and a half years old, dies. Later that year Nellie and her sister travel with their father to Mackay in Queensland where David Mitchell has business interests.

Meets Charles Nesbitt Frederick Armstrong, youngest son of Sir Andrew Armstrong, 1st baronet of Gallen Priory, King's County, Ireland.

22 December marries Charles Armstrong in Brisbane. Nellie is 21, Charles is three years older.

1883   George Armstrong born to Nellie at Marion Mill, Mackay.

1884   19 January leaves Mackay with George. Takes ship from Brisbane for Melbourne via Sydney.

17 May professional debut with Metropolitan Liedertafel at Melbourne Town Hall.

1886   11 March sails for England with George and Charles at her father's invitation, joining his entourage when he is appointed Victorian Commissioner to the Indian and Colonial Exhibition in London.

1 May arrives in London. Auditions for Sir Hubert Parry (of the Royal College of Music and Professor of Music at Oxford), Sir Arthur Sullivan (composer and collaborator with W.S. Gilbert in the Savoy operas), Alberto Randegger (of the Royal Academy of Music and the Royal College of Music, composer-conductor), Wilhelm Ganz (Jenny Lind's accompanist), Alfred Cellier (associate of the Savoy Theatre and assistant to Sullivan).

1 June first London public concert appearance. Failure. Later that year attempts audition with Carl Rosa (opera impresario), but he fails to appear. Sends Madame Elise Weidermann's Melbourne introductory letter to Madame Mathilde Marchesi in Paris. Shortly thereafter Nellie successfully auditions for Marchesi.

In December becomes a pupil of Marchesi and meets Maurice Strakosch, impresario, at a special Marchesi-sponsored recital and at Marchesi's urging signs a contract with him.

1887   9 October Strakosch drops dead in Paris and Nellie is released from the contract which would otherwise have prevented her career developing as it did.

13 October Using the name Madame Melba, Nellie makes her operatic debut at the Théâtre de la Monnaie in Brussels as Gilda in *Rigoletto*. Her career is successfully launched.

1888   24 May Debut at Covent Garden in the title role in *Lucia di Lammermoor.*

1889   8 May Paris debut as Ophélie in Thomas' *Hamlet.*

1890   Begins liaison with Louis Phillippe, Duc d'Orleans, then 20.

1891   Melba and the Duc visit Russia. Melba sings before the Tsar at St Petersberg. Charles Armstrong challenges the Duc to a duel. Scandal escalates.

1 November Charles Armstrong serves Melba with divorce papers.

1892   Divorce proceedings dropped. The Duc is sent to Africa.

1893   La Scala and American debuts

1894   Charles Armstrong takes George to America when Melba is declared an unfit mother. Melba is not notified of his whereabouts.

1900   Armstrong divorces Melba in Texas.

1902   17 September Melba reaches Brisbane on her first return visit to Australia. Concert tour follows.

1903   28 March John Norton, editor of *Truth* publishes his open letter against Melba.

1904   Melba makes first recordings.

1906   Oscar Hammerstein persuades Melba to star at his new opera house, the Manhattan, in New York, rival to the Met.

1907   2 January Melba's first appearance at the Manhattan as Violetta in *La Traviata.*

1911   First J.C. Williamson/Melba opera season.

Her home, Coombe Cottage completed by architect John Grainger, father of composer Percy Grainger, one of Melba's proteges.

1914   Begins wartime fundraising in Australia and America.

1915   12 April gives first lesson to women of her vocal school founded at the Albert Street Conservatorium, East Melbourne, then under the directorship of composer Fritz Hart.

1918   Created a Dame of the British Empire (DBE) for war relief work, not for services to music.

1919   12 May returns to Covent Garden in *La Bohème*.

1923   Meets Beverley Nichols, then 23. He became the ghost-writer of her memoirs.

1924   J.C. Williamson/Melba opera seasons. Nichols stays at Coombe Cottage.

13 October Farewell at His Majesty's Theatre, Melbourne. Autobiography *Melodies and Memories* published.

1926   8 June Covent Garden farewell. *The Melba Method* published. (Written with Fritz Hart and Mary Campbell).

Melba makes her last recordings.

1928   J.C. Williamson/Melba opera seasons. Melba appears only in concerts.

1931   23 February Melba dies of failed face-lift at St Vincents Hospital, Sydney. Her flag draped coffin is brought to Melbourne by train in a special viewing carriage enabling the crowds who waited at every station to see it. She lies in state at Scots Church, which her father had built and is mourned by thousands who line the route to the Lilydale Cemetery where she is buried. For many years women of her vocal school sing over her grave on the anniversary of her death, a custom recently revived.

The words reproduced in this text are from the following sources:

'Waltz Song' from *Roméo and Juliette* (Gounod), libretto Jules Barbier and Michel Carre (Fred Rullman Ed., New York, 1900), English translation by Leonard Radic; 'Spargi d'amaro pianto' from *Lucia di Lammermoor* (Donizetti) libretto Salvatore Cammerano (Fred Rullman ed., New York, 1900), trans. by L. Radic; 'Auld Lang Syne' (trad.) words by Robbie Burns; 'Sempre libera' and 'Liabiamo ne'lieti calici' from *La Traviata* (Verdi) libretto Francesco Maria Piave, (Fred Rullman ed., New York, 1900), trans by L. Radic; 'Caro nome' from *Rigoletto* (Verdi) libretto Francesco Maria Piave (Boosey and Co. ed., London, 1871), trans by L. Radic; 'Le temps des lilas' (Chausson) lyrics M. Boucher, English trans. by L. Radic; 'Coming Through the Rye' (trad.) words by Robbie Burns; 'Donde lieta usci' from *La Bohème* (Puccini) libretto Guiseppe Giacosa and Luigi Illica, (Ricordi and Co ed, New York 1917) trans. by L. Radic; 'Home Sweet Home' (Henry Bishop) lyrics John Howard Payne; 'By the Waters of Minnetonka' (Thurlow Lieurance) lyrics Louis Poterat, English by M. Cavanas (Theo Presser Co and Chappell and Co ed, 1914); 'Songs My Mother Taught Me' (Dvorak) lyrics Heyduk, trans. by Natalia Macfarran, (Alfred Lengnick and Co ed, London, c.1920); 'Addio' (Paolo Tosti) lyrics by F. Rizelli, trans. by G.T. Whyte-Melville (Ricordi and Co ed, 1903); 'Believe Me if all Those Endearing Young Charms' (trad.) words by Thomas Moore

Peach Melba was first performed by the Playbox Theatre Company at the Beckett Theatre at the CUB Malthouse, Melbourne on 8 June 1990 with the following cast:

MELBA	Helen Noonan
MELBA TWO	Robynne Bourne
ACCOMPANIST	Peter Locke
ACTOR	David Bonney

Directed by Malcolm Robertson
Designed by Anna French
Lighting by David Murray

ACKNOWLEDGEMENTS

Thanks to Pru Niedorf and Roy Jordan of the National Library of Australia; Joyce McGrath of Queen's Hall, State Library of Victoria; Dr Robin Smith of the Music Library, Baillieu Library, University of Melbourne; Frank Van Straten of the Performing Arts Museum, Melbourne; Graeme Clarke of the Victorian Music Theatre; Jacqueline Bourne, Ian Miller and Georgina Binns of the Victorian College of the Arts Library; Dr Carlo Cohn, Director of the Italian Cultural Institute; Helen Noonan, Phillip Nunn, George Dreyfus, Stephen Radic, Kim Durban and the Melbourne Theatre Company (for the Spoleto Festival reading); Malcolm Robertson (for the Playbox workshop); Carrillo Gantner; Leonard Radic for his translations; Franco Cavarra; Victoria Chance and Lin Bender.

CHARACTERS

MELBA, Melba the singer.

MELBA TWO, Melba's professional conscience. The same actor plays Madame Marchesi and Parry's secretary. She also plays the woman in scene sixteen and the voiceover in scene thirteen.

ACCOMPANIST, Plays all Melba's accompaniments and Ranegger as well as the man in scene sixteen.

ACTOR, plays men in Melba's life — David Mitchell; Pietro Cecchi; Charles Armstrong; Sir Hubert Parry; Sir Arthur Sullivan; Salvatore Marchesi; Louis Philippe Duc d'Orleans; Caruso; Escoffier; John Norton; Oscar Hammerstein; Beverly Nicholls.

SETTING

It is the night of Melba's final concert — her last farewell. In reality this was in 1930. In the play it is forever now. On a stage somewhere — anywhere — in an island of light, Melba sings, drifts in and out of the past, a black grand piano open behind her; her impeccable partner, the accompanist, a man for all seasons, attends. A man and a woman come and go — her history, her professional conscience.

Peach Melba is a full length work played without an interval.

SCENE ONE

PROLOGUE

In the dark the recording of MELBA'S *speech from the stage of Covent Garden at her farewell of 8 June 1926 is heard, scratchy, antique:*
  [Applause]
MELBA RECORDING: *And now there's only one more word to say, and that is farewell. I won't say goodbye because farewell is such a beautiful word. I am sure you all know that it's part of a prayer and means 'fare-thee-well,' which I wish you all and I feel sure that you wish me the same.*
  [Applause]

SCENE TWO

1930. 'The Waltz Song' from Gounod's Roméo et Juliette *is heard pre-recorded with* MELBA'S *voice as if it were an early* MELBA *recording, technically primitive, in period, but the sound is overcome by the live voice of* MELBA. *As the lights come up,* MELBA *is seen and heard bringing the past, the recorded, to life. She is on stage at her final concert, which is in its last moments. In full concert dress, glittering with diamonds, she stands in the traditional concert position in the bow of the open black grand piano. The accompanist seated at it is in white tie and tails. A pool of light defines this concert setting against the black.* MELBA TWO *is gradually lit as the aria continues. She, too, is in a pool of light against the black and in a defined space but closer to the audience than* MELBA. *She is dressed identically and is miming* MELBA'S *voice and gestures.*

Non! Non! je ne veux pas t'écouter plus
longtemps!
Laisse mon âme à son printemps.
Ah! Je veux vivre
Dans ce rêve qui m'enivre;
Ce jour encore
Douce flamme
Je te garde dans mon âme
Comme un trésor:
[Repeat: Je veux vivre Dans ce reve qui
m'enivre etc]
Cette ivresse
De jeunesse
Ne dure, hélas! qu'un jour!
Puis vient l'heure
Où l'on pleure
Le coeur cède à l'amour
Et le bonheur fuit sans retour
Ah! Je veux vivre
Dans ce rêve qui m'enivre;
Longtemps encore,
Douce flamme
Je te garde dans mon âme
Comme un trésor!
Loin de l'hiver morose
Laisse-moi sommeiller
Et respirer la rose
Avant de l'effeuiller.
Ah! Douce flamme,
Reste dans mon ame
Comme un doux tresor!
Longtemps encor!
Ah!

[No! No! I'll no longer listen to you
Let my soul enjoy its spring.
Ah! I want to live
This dream which enraptures me.
Still this day
Sweet flame
I keep you in my soul
Like a treasure:
[Repeat: I want to live this dream which en-
raptures me etc]
Alas, this youthful rapture
Lasts but a day.
Then comes the time
Of tearfulness;
The heart gives way to love
And happiness flees, never to return.
Ah! I want to live
This dream which enraptures me!
For a long time yet
Sweet flame
I keep you in my heart
Like a treasure.
Far from the gloomy winter
Let me slumber
And breathe of the rose
Before I strip it of its petals.
Ah! Sweet flame,
Stay in my heart
Like a precious treasure,
For a long while yet!
Ah!]

SCENE THREE

The two Melbas and the accompanist freeze in mid-phrase.

MELBA TWO: Now!

MELBA: I can't!

MELBA TWO: You promised you'd . . .

MELBA: . . . I'd go. When the time came. I'd . . .

MELBA TWO: . . . You'd go. Gracefully.

MELBA: . . . Once more. Just *once* more.

MELBA TWO: No!

MELBA: Please! If I don't sing I'll die.

MELBA TWO: Rubbish! Find something . . . a new man.
. . a . . .

MELBA: an encore. A last . . .

MELBA TWO: [*unfreezing to look impatiently at her fob watch, and nodding at the pianist*] He's on union time remember . . .

MELBA: [*unfreezing*] You're a hard woman.

MELBA TWO: [*smug*] So they say.

MELBA: It's always pounds shillings and pence!

MELBA TWO: [*sarcastic*] Are those diamonds new?

MELBA: I don't need diamonds. [*Indicating the audience*] *They* do. They *need* to see me like this.

MELBA TWO: So do you. It's the price of success. And you've paid it.

MELBA: I've paid a price. Thanks to *you*. I gave up everything because of you. I wanted to be a *woman*.

MELBA TWO: I may think like a man. I have to. But it didn't put *you* into trousers. Is that what you *wanted* to be — your father's son?

MELBA: I'm the *best* of my father's sons.

MELBA TWO: Or — more than the *best* of daughters?

MELBA: I *wanted* to please him, yes, all my life, but —
[*Both burst into the cadenza of the Waltz Song as* DAVID MITCHELL *enters. He is a Scot with a Forfarshire accent, a bluff, stern Presbyterian patriarch. He cuts the two* MELBAS *short.*]

SCENE FOUR

MITCHELL: I'll not have it!

MELBA: Oh *won't* you!

 [MELBA *sings a handful of emphatic notes from the cadenza, furious.*]

MITCHELL: No man of feeling will suffer his wife, his sister, *or* his daughter to become a public singer or performer of any description who has any other means of providing for her. It is the hard weapon of necessity alone that will induce women of delicacy to appear before the public for *hire!* It's agin the Bible!

MELBA: The *Bible*? Matthew Five, verse fifteen: 'Neither do men light a candle and put it under a bushel, but upon a candlestick and it giveth light unto all that are in the house. Let your light so shine before men.'

MITCHELL: The devil is known to quote scripture.

MELBA: God gave me this voice, not the devil. I have a duty to use it. In *public!*

MITCHELL: Your duty lies at home. To your mother. *And* to me. And soon enough now ye'll belong to the man you marry.

MELBA: *Belong?* To a *man?*

MITCHELL: You belong first to the domesticities, and *next* to the region outside your front door.

MELBA: I'll run away.

MITCHELL: And ruin your reputation? Ye've no money but mine. Ye canna leave your home without permission. And ye'll not presume to ask it till all your duties there are done. And *then* only to do good works and attend sober functions.

MELBA: I won't be buried alive. I *know* what I'm worth.

MITCHELL: You've got a girl's foolish ambitions, Nellie. It's time to grow up now. No *real* woman thinks of herself first. ·

MELBA: If I have to think of everyone else's needs before mine I won't be a *real* woman, I'll be *dead!* There's lessons. And costumes — I *need* those fees and you know it.

MITCHELL: If you insist on it ye'll be *forcing* me to see you don't want by it.

[*She attempts to interject but is silenced.*]

If I don't pay up it'll look as if I'm either too poor to support you or too much of a miser to oblige you.

[*She again attempts to interject but is silenced.*]

And that'd bring down my credit in the building trade.

[*She turns her back on him and defiantly whistles. 'You Should See Me Dance The Polka'*]

You could be the *ruin* of me, Nellie Mitchell! And stop that infernal noise. A whistling hen is good for neither God nor men. You'll oblige me by remembering just who it is that's ruling *this* roost, my girl!

[MITCHELL *exits.*]

SCENE FIVE

MELBA *sings, the Cadenza of the Mad Scene from Donizetti's* Lucia di Lammermoor. PIETRO CECCHI, *MELBA's singing teacher for seven years and* MELBA TWO, *sit before* MELBA *on little gilt chairs as an audience. He is an Italian tenor, an ex-member of the Lyster opera company. He soon takes over the teacher role, interrupting* MELBA.

CECCHI: So. This Charlie — this — this *man!* First you are in love, then not. Now you are married and now you're not. First there is no baby, then there is. Now you give up singing, then you want me to form a concert party for you to make money and a *career!* Such letters from — from —

[*He searches for and finds a letter.*]

MELBA: Mackay! Maestro Cecchi.

CECCHI: He is in Mackay?

MELBA: I sincerely hope so but I can't help looking over my shoulder all the time.

CECCHI: What sort of thing *is* he?

MELBA: You should see his — thighs.

CECCHI: [*understanding*] Ah! And your father?

MELBA: We're not speaking.

CECCHI: But he was there, in Brisbane, when you marry!

MELBA: He's abandoned me — not socially, you understand — financially. For making my bed in a hurry *and* lying in it. It's not fair, Maestro. You men get away with it, but me — all I got was George.

CECCHI: He's a *beautiful* baby. Go back to Queensland. Be a wife, be a mother — and stop tormenting me.

MELBA: There's no-one to sing to up there. I need a *real* audience. I *need* to know *who* I am, not just how good I am! I could run my own business affairs as well as my father. I had a good teacher *there*. But I need capital. And I need to advertise. *Now*. If I can't let rip soon I'll go mad!

   [*The pianist plays the final section of the Allegro of the Mad Scene from Donizetti's* Lucia di Lammermoor.]

CECCHI: [*swept up by her voice, giving in to her, a sudden about face, excitedly over the music*] Yes, go mad! Where you belong — on the stage. You are a *voice!* Vocal cords, lungs — only organs. Is *this* your organ? [*Hands hovering over her pubes*] Too unreliable. Or this? [*Music starts. He touches her head*] Too calculating. *All* of you — that is your organ. A total instrument, with all the colours of the organ you play in church, that you *feel*, in here. [*Thumping his own chest*] Now — from the *biggest* pipes! Control! Power!

MELBA: [*sending herself up by replacing the text of the last six bars with:*] Ah! No, not to Queens — land, and not with Charlie!

   [*They collapse in laughter.*]

CECCHI: It's no joke, Nellie Armstrong. I may be only your teacher but I am also your friend. I will help — I *know* people. Your father is a difficulty, yes, but worst of all is this, this — husband. What good is he to you? A little joy to begin, eh? But *now!* Get rid of him!

MELBA: He's mostly brawn and bad temper and — lord help us — the only music he likes is Gilbert and Sullivan.

CECCHI: But there is a title. *Very* attractive. Very — *useful.*

MELBA: Very remote. He was a horse trader when I met him. He can ride anything on four legs *or* two, damn him.

CECCHI: This big sugar plantation, surely —

MELBA: He's only the manager.

CECCHI: [*suddenly enlightened*] To support you! Now I see. It is not going good. So he drinks. And the wages go, and —

MELBA: [*revealing the worst*] Signor Cecchi, someone told tales out of turn. So now he's not sure if he had me hot off the press.

CECCHI: Your father — *that's* why he's angry?

MELBA: [*she shrugs*] Not much chance of getting *him* to foot the bills. We were still in mourning for my mother when he took us up north, you might remember. Belle and I didn't mind Daddy being off all day on business on the site for the new mill, but what did he expect? It was hot and we were bored and — there was Charlie.

[*The pianist begins the Moderato introduction of fifteen bars before 'Spargi d'amaro pianto' from Donizetti's* Lucia di Lammermoor.]

One day I may forget his face, but how do I forget the feel of him? I'll *never* be rid of Kangaroo Charlie.

SCENE SIX

She picks up her music from the piano and comes in with the first bar of 'Spargi d'amaro pianto.'

Spargi d'amaro pianto,
Il mio terrestre velo,
Mentre lassù nel cielo,

Io pregherò, pregherò per te.
Al giunger tuo soltanto,
Fia bello il ciel per me!

[Ah, shed your tears of sorrow
Upon my earthly garment!
In Heaven above
I will pray for you,
Though only when you join me
Will Heaven be bliss for me!]

[The actor is now CHARLIE, *who makes love to her.*
She persists in singing instead of responding so he
takes the music from her. A clash of wills ensues.
At the downward run of the bar before the Pui
mosso, CHARLIE *loses his temper and tears up the*
music. MELBA *loses her temper. They fight for the*
duration of the Piu mosso 's unvocalised passage.
They shout at one another.]

CHARLIE: You'll get no applause from *me!*

MELBA: I'll make do with the sound of rain on the roof.
And *it* never ceases in this God-forsaken place.

CHARLIE: Your *place* is here.

MELBA: All *you* want is another servant. I'm not one of
your Kanaks.

CHARLIE: You took a vow of obedience.

MELBA: I'll take a new one — no man is ever going to
rule *me* with his rod again.

[Triumphant, she joins the accompanist at the third last
bar of the Piu mosso at 'Ah!' and takes up the refrain
in the repeat at a faster tempo than given. MELBA
packs the 'baby' — a roll of clothes — in a case, with
the torn-up music and CHARLIE'S *hat, which he has*
discarded during the fight. She clutches the hat, panic
struck at the loss of him, then makes love to the hat
as if it were CHARLIE, *then turns against him, enraged,*
and stamps the hat underfoot. She packs the hat and
closes the case. At the last minute, she takes the hat
out and hurls it offstage, bowling it like a cricket ball.
CHARLIE *exits.* MELBA *collapses in tears.]*

SCENE SEVEN

MELBA TWO: Stop that! Crying over a *man?* What weakness. Be angry — it helps the performance.

MELBA: [*recovering*] I'm not crying over Charlie. I'm crying because — that sort of thing — is over.

MELBA TWO: Not if I know *you.* Come on now, — the facelift will do wonders. You'll look —

MELBA: I'll *feel* like old wine in a new bottle.

MELBA TWO: The voice, though —

TOGETHER: — pure, perfect, like a boy's, but —

MELBA: A thousand little towns! A thousand farewells! It *used* to be the custom, but divas don't collect their pensions like *this* anymore.

MELBA TWO: *You, a pension?*

MELBA: Am I making a fool of myself?

MELBA TWO: Without a doubt.

MELBA: Does it matter?

MELBA TWO: It will when you're dead.

MELBA: You want the silence of the grave *now?*

MELBA TWO: I want a little dignity. *Before* and after. Are you afraid?

MELBA: I keep remembering. Things I can't alter. Things that play themselves over and over, needle caught in the groove at the most unexpected moments, picking up — things — anywhere, suddenly dumping me down, mid-aria in scenes I've already played a million times. *Only —*

MELBA TWO: Only now there are things you'd forgotten. Small things, of no importance. You begin to wonder *why.* What do they mean?

MELBA: I'd forgotten that Charlie tore up the music.

MELBA TWO: Did he break the chairs?

MELBA: My father didn't know about the boys and the river. If he had . . . !

MELBA TWO: Wasn't it your sister — Belle . . . who?

MELBA: It was *Mother* who objected to my whistling.

MELBA TWO: That was at school.

MELBA: Was it my humming?

MELBA TWO: Some things you *refuse* to remember. You fight against it, won't face it, but in the end —. The day Charlie tried to drown you, out there in the little boat, getting away from the heat, sailing. When the wind changed —

MELBA: — and it came, this long wave, out of nowhere, from a horizon we couldn't see, out of the stillness. We'd quarrelled. There was this — push. From behind. He said later, it was the sail slapping, out of control, that I'd let go the rope as the wave took us, that I hadn't heard him yelling at me to —. I fell, — and —.

MELBA TWO: Just as *well* he didn't know you could swim like that.

MELBA: It was the tide — we didn't know — we —

MELBA TWO: You quarrelled. Over — George. Gossip. And there we have it, eh? The great lover doubting if he was —. You were in such a hurry to get married.

MELBA: No!

MELBA TWO: Yes. But some things *are* best forgotten.

MELBA: Like Cecchi?

MELBA TWO: That *had* to be done. It was — expedient.

MELBA: I owed him so much and I —

SCENE EIGHT

CECCHI *presents his bill for lessons to* MELBA

CECCHI: *This* is what you owe me.

MELBA: I owe you nothing.

CECCHI: You owe me *everything*. You also owe me eighty guineas.

MELBA: I haven't got it.

CECCHI: Who arranged your concerts? I *know* what you've earned this year — seven hundred and fifty pounds.

MELBA: Clothes. Music.

CECCHI: And the invisible husband? You keep your purse shut to him and pay your debt to me or I will take my tuition bill and present it to your father. *He* will say it is disgraceful not to pay. And maybe he will think twice about taking you to England with him. The state commissioner to the great colonial exhibition trailing a scandal about his daughter? I think not.

MELBA: You'll get your money.

CECCHI: No, Nellie. You don't understand me. I don't want your money. I want you to repay your *debt*. To me. To the man who created you.

MELBA: *Created* me? Nellie Mitchell created Dame Nellie Melba. I owe you *nothing*. *None* of you. I am what I am in *spite* of you.

MELBA TWO: In spite of your father? You wrote in the memoirs: 'Throughout my life there has been one man who meant more than all others, one man for whose praise I thirsted, whose character I have tried to copy — my father.'

CECCHI: You are a good imitation. *Very* good. You're as mean and close-fisted as he was.

MELBA: He was never like that with *me!*

MELBA TWO: No? What happened to Vere?

MELBA: I went to sleep. In front of the fire. And my little sister died *because* I went to sleep. She didn't look *really* ill. Children can seem worse than they are. When I woke up — she — I should have known. It was the middle of the night but I should have insisted on a doctor.

MELBA TWO: You did.

MELBA: No.

MELBA TWO: To your father. He said not to be foolish. And next day he went to his business as usual saying to wait. You did nothing because he ordered it. Doctors cost money. Like teachers. You think he killed Vere. With your help.

MELBA: [*to* CECCHI] Here. [*Throwing her purse at him*] *Take* your eighty guineas.

    [*He takes it, counts the contents, pockets it, and hands back the purse which* MELBA *refuses.*]

CECCHI: I'll be back for the rest.

MELBA: You'll get what you deserve from me — silence.
I will refuse to acknowledge you were ever my teacher.

CECCHI: If you turn your back on me now don't expect
to be welcomed when you come home. And one day
you will *want* to come home.

[MELBA *sings, ironically, a verse of* Auld Lang Syne
*'Should old acquaintance be forgot and never brought
to mind? Should old acquaintance be forgot and the
days of Old Lang Syne'*]

SCENE NINE

*Ships whistle, a crowd on a wharf, carriage wheels, as
all reposition. We are in London. To a metronome
beating* MELBA *sings the opening phrase of the 'Sempre
libera,' section of 'Ah, fors'e lui' from Verdi's* La
Traviata. *She is cut short by the accompanist who sighs,
turns a page and calls:*]

ACCOMPANIST: Next! [*Then turns off the metronome.*
[SIR HUBERT PARRY *is dictating a letter to his lady
secretary. He is big, pompous, languorous,
patronising and aware of his status as a renowned
teacher and composer.*]

PARRY: Dear Miss — *is* it Miss? No — Dear *Mrs*
Armstrong. I have received your letter of introduction
and I am sure it is possible you are everything our
mutual — *acquaintance* — says you are. Alas you are
only one of hundreds who wish to be heard by me. I
must decline the pleasure, yours etcetera etcetera,
Hubert Parry, Royal College and all that. Oh dear —
all these *Girls*. What am I to *do* with the excess? I
charge double and *still* they come. My time is *full*.
It's given me quite a headache.
[*The accompanist plays a note which* MELBA *sings.
He is* ALBERTO RANDEGGER, *opera composer* —

*conductor. Very chic, charming, quick, flighty and in
love with himself. He's barely listened.*]

RANDEGGER: [*played by the accompanist*] Wonderful!
You may tell everyone that Randegger, *the* great
composer, *the* great conductor, has heard you and says
so. It will open doors! But — [*Shrugging elegantly*]
— I have no time. Come back later. Maybe next year
. . .

[*The metronome ticks. The two* MELBAS *pace, and
consult their fob watches*]

MELBA: Enough! He's not coming.

MELBA TWO: Bloody foreigner! I *saw* him pencil this
appointment on his cuff.

MELBA: What did he do — send me *and* the memo to the
laundry?

MELBA TWO: Who *cares* about Carl Rosa and his piddling
little company *anyway?* Two hours waiting's —

TOGETHER: Enough!

[*The metronome ceases. They snap the watches shut
as* SIR ARTHUR SULLIVAN *of Gilbert and Sullivan fame
opens his watch as he sits at the piano by the
pianist. He is very bored.*]

SULLIVAN: Next. [*He puts the watch in sight.*]

MELBA *repeats the opening phrase of 'Sempre Libera'
getting further this time. Sullivan isn't listening but
beats out a quite different rhythm on the piano edge
with his hand, thinking to himself and talking to the
pianist.* MELBA *looks expectant. He keeps on
beating. She coughs.*]

Yes Mrs Armstrong. That is *alright*. I'm afraid there are
no vacancies in the Savoy Opera Company at the moment,
but after you have studied some more, say for a year or
so, Mr Gilbert and I might, — just *might*, you understand,
find a little something for you in one of our *best* pieces.
In *The Mikado* perhaps.

[*With the accompanist he plays 'Three pretty Maids
From School unwary, straight from a ladies' seminary,
freed from the genus tutelary, three pretty maids from
school' from* The Mikado.]

HOW PEACH MELBA BEGAN

I first "met" Dame Nellie Melba when I played Melba in *Manning Clark's History of Australia - the Musical*. Part of the research I undertook for the role was to read Thérèse Radic's marvellous biography of Melba. When *History* closed early I decided to do what many out-of-work actors do and *make* some work. So I approached Therese Radic to write me a script in which I could sing some of the loveliest of the songs associated with this most famous of Australia's women artists. Grants came from the Australia Council, the Victorian Ministry for the Arts and MTC who included the first draft of *Peach Melba* (then known as *Melba's Last Farewell*) in the Spoleto Play-reading series of 1988. The script was further developed with assistance from the ANZ Trustees and the VSO - to all of those organisations, thanks.

Melba has appeal for me for many reasons - she was and remains a great Australian woman, an achiever whose qualities of resilience and determination are inspiring. Above all she was, and remains, a supreme artist.

Helen Noonan

AUTHOR'S NOTE

A play on Melba was the last thing I had in mind when Helen Noonan came to me to commission *Peach Melba* three years ago. I was still in the recovery stage after publishing *Melba: The Voice of Australia*, a biography commissioned by Bill Reed, then publisher at Macmillan and himself a playwright, and a book that Helen had read and which sent her to look for me. In neither case did I set out on the task willingly, let alone because I felt some compulsion to put the record straight about a national heroine - and Melba was certainly once that, and as certainly had been wrongfully deposed.

What was irresistable about both the book and the play was a chance to do something I had never done before and to do it, in both cases, with a great deal of support and faith in what I could do. That doesn't happen often for me and I respond delightedly when it does.

The problem was to devise a play with music from the Melba repertoire as its core and not merely as decoration. Helen is an actor-singer and she wanted scope for both vocations, though not with one at the expense of the other. I wanted arias and songs which could symbolise the crisis points of the life, and a text that built up to, used, and quit those points organically. I wanted to look at the life from the perspective of looming death, at the career - a fabulously successful one by any standards - from the point of view of culmination, at the woman in old age realising what must be left unresolved. For this I had to avoid realism and create a style that would reflect the way the mind swings, rapid and fragmented, back and forth over time, place and events.

At the moment of farewell, then, Melba is haunted by visions of the critical moments of her past, moments that are sometimes ugly, sometimes beautiful, often sad. She questions, judges, relives the long years of struggle and of triumph and sees the cost she has willingly paid to be the Assoluta.

It is this image of Melba as the successful careerist coming to full term, still trailing the loves and hates, the fears and regrets of women, never losing touch with her humanity but haunted by this transitoriness, that informs the play. The music is intergral to this view.

Thérèse Radic
Playwright

David Bonney

Robynne Bourne

Graham Clarke

DAVID BONNEY

David studied with the School of Drama at the Victorian College of the Arts and graduated in 1987. His work since then includes *Les Liasons Dangereuse, Romeo and Juliet*, and *As You Like It* for the MTC. In 1989 he appeared in STC'S *Romeo and Juliet, Stroke* for the Chamber Made Opera Company and Peter King's production *Ursurper of the Plains*. David's television credits include *The Flying Doctors* and *This Man This Woman* for Crawford Productions. David played one of the lead roles in Lawrence Johnston's film *Night Out* which has been selected for screening at the 1990 Cannes Film Festival.

ROBYNNE BOURNE

Robynne has worked at the Nimrod and Jane Street Theatres in Sydney, and the Lighthouse Company in Adelaide where she appeared in many productions including *Midsummer Night's Dream, Twelfth Night, Blood Wedding, Pal Joey*, and *Silver Lining*. For the Melbourne Theatre Company she has appeared in *Too Young for Ghosts, Never In My Lifetime, One Day of the Year, She Stoops To Conquer*, and *The Entertainer*. In 1989 she appeared in the Playbox production of *Nice Girls* at the Theatre Royal in Hobart.

GRAHAM CLARKE

Graham is well known as a musical director, conductor, accompanist and coach with major theatre companies ranging form J.C Williamson's and the Trust to the Adelaide Festival Trust and the MTC. He is equally well known for his work in opera and ballet. He is a trained dancer as well as having majored in both piano and voice, holding the Eric and Lynda Jullian Memorial Scholarship at the University of Melbourne. His success over the last two decades as a teacher led him to focus on his private teaching practice with students in every sphere of the profession both in Australia and overseas. At the moment he is also involved in formalising his research through post-graduate studies.

Anna French   Peter Locke   David Murray

ANNA FRENCH

Anna received a Diploma of Art from Prahran Technical College and worked with the MTC after graduating. She has since been Resident Designer with the State Theatre Company of South Australia and the National Theatre in Perth. She has also had strong links with the West Australian Ballet Company. During her time in Perth she received the National Theatre Critics Award for Best Designer and the following year was awarded the London Sainthill Design Scholarship which allowed her to study in Europe and Great Britain. Her work includes *The Last of the Knucklemen* for the State Theatre Company of South Australia (directed by David Williamson) and *The Man from Mukinupin* for the MTC. Past work for Playbox includes *Not About Heroes, The Father We Loved On The Beach By The Sea* (Directed by Malcolm Robertson), and *A Long Day's Journey Into Night*.

PETER LOCKE

Peter studied Classics at Kings College, Cambridge; solo piano at the Royal Academy of Music, London; and piano accompaniment at L'Accademia di Santa Cecilia, Rome. After a year's touring world-wide with a chamber music ensemble, he gave up music for the theatre. For seven years he was an actor in revue, straight theatre and television in England and Italy. Returning to music, he was awarded a scholarship at Teatro "La Fenice" in Venice, one of Italy's historic opera houses. He stayed there for ten years. He has subsequently worked in many opera houses including the VSO and as an accompanist and teacher for Hans Werner Hewze, the late Tito Gobbi and Elisabeth Schwarzkopf. His most recent work was as Chorus Master and recitalist in Iceland.

DAVID MURRAY

David moved to Melbourne from Sydney after touring here with Jill Perryman's *Leading Lady* in 1974. Since then he has worked as a Stage Manager, Production Manager, Head Electrician, Technical Director, Theatre Consultant and Lighting Designer with most of the major Australian theatre, opera and ballet companies. His work as lighting designer includes *Carmen, The Snow Queen* and *The Magic Flute* for VSO, *Circus Oz* at the Edinburgh Festival 1987 and 1988, the Dublin Milennium Festival and the Site Lighting Design for Expo 88 in Brisbane. Previous lighting designs for Playbox include *A Bed Of Roses, Long Day's Journey Into Night, Antigone, Extremities, A Spring Song, Beyond Therapy* and *Riff Raff the Remix*.

Helen Noonan   *Thérèse Radic*   *Malcolm Robertson*

HELEN NOONAN

Helen is a graduate of the National Theatre Drama School and has studied singing with Graham Clarke since 1982. She has appeared in roles as varied as Violetta in Verdi's *La Traviata* and Ariel in *The Tempest*. For the MTC Helen has appeared in *Victoria Bitter* and *Sweeney Todd* and in the National Tour of *Pirates Of Penzance* for the VSO. Helen's most recent role has been as Ghost of Opera in the acclaimed *Recital* for Chamber Made Opera, having completed successful seasons at Anthill and Universal Theatres in 1989 and at Belvoir St in 1990. Helen Noonan commissioned the writing of *Peach Melba* in 1988.

THÉRÈSE RADIC - PLAYWRIGHT

Thérèse Radic's background in theatre and music is extensive. She has a PhD in Australian Music History and has written three music biographies: G.W.L. *Marshall-Hall: Portrait of a Lost Crusader'*; *Bernard Heinze*; and *Melba: The Voice of Australia*. MTC produced her play *Some Of My Best Friends Are Women* in 1976, which she co-wrote with Leonard Radic. Past works with Playbox include *A Whip Round for Percy Grainger* and *Madame Mao*, which, after a successful season in Melbourne, was later produced in Sydney, the UK and the USA. Thérèse's play about Dame Nellie Melba, origininally named *Melba's Last Farewell*, was given a public reading by MTC in 1988's Spoleto Festival. In 1989 Playbox workshopped the play thus enabling the script to be finalised and produced. Thérèse currently does sessional lecturing on Australian music in Monash University's Music Department, where she is an Australian Research Council scholar researching and writing a history of music in Australia.

MALCOLM ROBERTSON - DIRECTOR

Malcolm began his career in theatre thirty nine years ago. He was a founding member of the Union Theatre Repertory Company (MTC) and the Australian Elizabethan Theatre Trust Drama Company. Malcolm was first Theatre Consultant with the Australia Council. He has been closely associated with the development of the Playbox Theatre Company and is now the Playbox Literary Manager. Recently Malcolm has directed *Mark Twain Down Under* for Playbox, Alex Buzo's *Stingray* at La Mama, and last year *The Entrepreneurs* at Courthouse. As an actor he has appeared in *Volpone* (the Church), *Benny Wallis Meets his Maker* (Playbox), *The Imaginary Invalid* (Anthill), *Farmyard* (La Mama), and *On Edge* (Universal). His film and TV credits include *The Last Wave, Kangaroo, The Lancaster Miller Affair, True Believers, The Year My Voice Broke*, and *Vietnam*. He will be seen in John Duigan's film *Flirting* and the tele-movie *Bony* later this year.

Many Happy Returns

to all Red Cross Blood Donors

We need you
back and back and back

For further information phone 616 0300

Theatre Centre of Monash University

Board of Directors
Graeme Samuel (Chairman), Professor Mal Logan (Deputy Chairman), Tony Adair, Sandra Bardas, Tom Dery, Rhonda Galbally, Helen Nugent, Peter Wade

Artistic Director	Carrillo Gantner
General Manager	Jill Smith
Production Manager	Robert Taylor
Secretary to Artistic Director	Pam Barden
Marketing Manager	Ross Mollison
Publicity Coordinator	Ruth Tedder
Literary Manager	Malcolm Robertson
Stage Manager	Ross Murray
Workshop Manager	Colin Orchard
Wardrobe Supervisor	Robin Hall
Education Liaison Officer	Camilla Gold
Composer in Residence	Stuart Greenbaum
Graphic Design	Steve Malpass of
	Malpass & Burrows
Trainee Carpenter	Anthea Parsons

PLAYBOX THEATRE CENTRE SPONSORS 1990

The Board, Artists and Staff of the Playbox Theatre Centre would like to thank:
The Victorian Government through the Ministry for the Arts for a general grant.
The Performing Arts Board of the Australia Council for a general grant.

The Literature and Performing Arts Boards of the Australia Council for project support for our 1990
Literary Manager, and Commissioning and Workshops programmes.
The Performing Arts Board of the Australia Council for project support for our 1990/91
Trainee Carpenter.
The Age
Channel 7
Monash University

THE BECKETT SEASON
Sponsored by The Red Cross Blood Bank
Funded by The Victorian Health Promotion Foundation

Victorian
Ministry for
the Arts.

THE MERLYN SEASON
The Victorian Health Promotion Foundation and 'Mahler Vienna and the Twentieth Century'
ANZ
For Peach Melba

Mitchelton Vintners for premium wines
Puttocks of 105 Bridport Street, Albert Park for great hair care
Australian Airlines; the official domestic airline of the Playbox Theatre Centre

PLAYBOX
presents

The World Premiere of

Peach Melba

by Thérèse Radic

CAST

MELBA	Helen Noonan
MELBA TWO	Robynne Bourne
ACTOR	Daivd Bonney
ACCOMPANIST	Peter Locke

DIRECTOR	Malcolm Robertson
SET AMD COSTUME DESIGN	Anna French
LIGHTING DESIGNER	David Murray
PRODUCTION MANAGER	Robert Taylor
STAGE MANAGER	Ross Murray
WARDROBE SUPERVISOR	Robin Hall
ADDITIONAL COSTUMES	Blair Broadhurst
SOUND EFFECTS	Stuart McKenzie
	Stuart Greenbaum
SET CONSTRUCTION	Colin Orchard
	Anthea Parsons

The writing of this play - *Peach Melba* - originated from an idea by Helen Noonan who commissioned Thérèse Radic to write an original play with funding grants from the Melbourne Theatre Company, the Australia Council and the Victorian Ministry for the Arts. Grateful acknowledgement is made in particular to Charitable Trusts (ANZ Trustees) and also to the Victoria State Opera for their facilitation of further script development.

SPECIAL THANKS

Graham Clarke, Roy Baldwin, Vincent Kiss, Tony White, Blair Edgar, Lise Rodgers, Andrew Murrell, Joan Harris, John Jory, Kim Durban, Jean McQuarrie, Performing Arts Museum, Coles Myer Archives, Melbourne University Sports Centre, the *Truth*, Douglas Horton and Chamber Made, John Weis, Tanya Hamby.

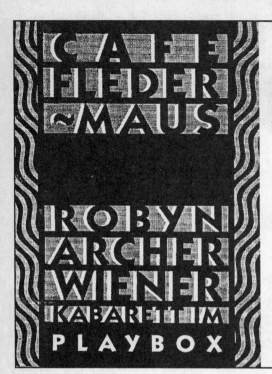

**CAFE FLEDERMAUS -
NOW PLAYING
IN**

THE MERLYN

**A STUNNINGLY
BEAUTIFUL NEW
THEATRE
UNTIL JUNE 16
685 5111 or BASS**

**FROM
JUNE 20 TO JUNE 30
THE ALEXANDER THEATRE
MONASH UNIVERSITY
565 3992**

ALEXANDER THEATRE
MONASH UNIVERSITY

JUNE BRONHILL
IN
NUNSENSE
June 7th to 16th

ROBYN ARCHER
IN
CAFE FLEDERMAUS
June 20th to 30th

FOR BOOKINGS & ENQUIRIES
565-3992

'They were served at precisely the right temperature. So were the oysters.'

CUC77 APB11220-A

Crown Lager. Australia's finest.

National Australia **Bank**

is proud to be a
principal sponsor
of the
Malthouse Theatre Complex

SCENE TEN

1886. DAVID MITCHELL *storms at* MELBA.

MITCHELL: You'll not get another penny, I tell you. Ye've
had long enough to prove yer worth and look what's
come of it — nothing but bills. And now it's Paris
you want. If Madame Marchesi says no to you ye're to
come home with me and there's to be an end to it.

MELBA: And if she says yes?

MITCHELL: I'll give ye what'll keep you decent and no
more. *And* your sister to keep an eye on you. That
husband of yours'll not be any use to you, that's for
sure. *He'll* stay with his regiment and his horses and
just as well. Your mother-in-law's not a bad sort of a
woman, but the rest of 'em are high and mighty. The
gentry won't take kindly to having an opera singer in
the family so you'll not disgrace me by going to *them*.
A year, that's all I'll give ye. Then it's either fetch
for yourself or —

MELBA: If I have to accept a second class ticket from you
today I'll travel first class the rest of my life. Oh, I'll
fetch for myself alright.

SCENE ELEVEN

The accompanist hands her a letter. MATHILDE MARCHESI,
*the greatest teacher of her day, but now in need of a
great new pupil, speaks the letter* MELBA *reads.* MARCHESI
is old, imperious, regal, a martinet.

MARCHESI: You may come to us. We will listen. Some
rules. You will work eight hours a day. Not with the
voice — with the head. And we will see.
  [MELBA *sings a triumphant snatch of the end of
  'Sempre libera', finishing as if in Paris auditioning*

for MARCHESI *in her studio.* MARCHESI, *apparently unaffected, is in a state of suppressed excitement.*]
Why do you screech your top notes? Can't you sing *piano?*

[MELBA *sings a soft top B*]
Higher!

[MARCHESI *strikes top C on the piano.* MELBA *sings it softer still, then on alone and softer to D, then to E.* MARCHESI, *barely controlled, imperious, rounds on her.*]
Mrs Armstrong, — are you serious?

MELBA: I've never been more serious in my life.

MARCHESI: Alors. Before you start to learn anything you will have to *un*learn *everything.* The chest notes are too high so you force the voice. Change to middle notes on F. Begin the head notes on F sharp. Once on the head notes, *always practise pianissimo. If* you are serious, and *if* I permit you to study with me for one year, I will make something *extra-ordinary of you.*

[MELBA *bursts into tears.*]
[*Exasperated.*] Oh, yes, tears. I offend you? So be it. You wish to go?

MELBA: [*hardening to match her.*] No. Never.

MARCHESI: [*revealing the great secret*] So many students. So many *ingrates!* De Murska, Calve, Eames, Mary Garden — once at the top and they deny me. *Me!* They say I make teachers now, not singers. But *you.* Obey me and for you — everything. Teach — introduce — influence — I will pay for the debut — *but!* Before Marchesi, no-one. And thereafter no-one *but* Marchesi. Always — *always—* to acknowledge your debt. Agreed?

MELBA: Agreed.

MARCHESI: [*letting go at last and rushing off to find her husband*] Salvatore, at *last* I have a star!

Sempre libera degg'io
folleggiare di gioia in gioia,
vo'che scorra il viver mio
pei sentieri del piacer.

Nasca il giorno, o il giorno mouia,
sempre lieta ne' ritrovi,
a diletti sempre nuovi
dee volare il mio pensier.

[Free forever must I be
to flit from pleasure to pleasure,
to taste of life's delights,
First one and then another.
As each day dawns, as each day dies,
Ever happy I'll discover
Fresh delights to set
My spirits soaring.]

[Exit. MELBA *resumes 'Sempre libera'. Monsieur le Marquis, i.e. SALVATORE MARCHESI, MATHILDE'S husband, an aged Italian baritone and comic figure, enters hurriedly, struggling excitedly to adjust his state of undress. As* MELBA *climaxes with the penultimate note of the descending run, he faints.* MELBA *goes to help him.]*

SALVATORE: Where am I? Where is my wife? Il pezzo da novanta?

MELBA: Shall I go for help, Monsieur le Marquis.

SALVATORE: It is I who need help, not *you! Where* is my wife. What have I done to be deserted like this? There I was with Le Figaro in the smallest room — reading, you understand, not using. I meant to have a bath but I am storing my boots in it at the moment and in she comes. In! Shouting about a star! Such indignity! And drags me out, only one half dressed of me. And she is *right!* What is your name?

MELBA: Nellie Armstrong.

SALVATORE: *[holding his ears]* Barbarous! Where do you come from?

MELBA: Melbourne.

SALVATORE: This is a very Italian place, no? Only Italians are taken seriously for opera, yes? Ah, Madame Melbournaria?

MELBA: Good God, no. . . How about plain Melba?

SALVATORE: I must find Mathilde. You must begin at once. [*He exits.* MELBA *sings wordless vocalises from the* Marchesi Method, *then begins to add words of her own. She is practising.*]

MELBA: [*singing*] . . .money, money, money, money. Success, success, success, success. Danger, danger, danger, danger. Charlie's coming, coming, coming, coming. He's mad, mad, mad, mad, mad, mad. Mad. Will he try to ruin me? Me, me. Me, me, me? I'll kill, kill, kill, kill, him first. What's he *want?* Money, money, money, money, money's running out.

SALVATORE: [*rushing in, frantic*] Madame! Madame! Strakosch is here — Strakosch! The godfather of godfathers! Mathilde will commit murder! *He* will murder Mathilde! We must call the police! No — we must hide! No — we must run away. Incognito. Now!

MELBA: What on earth for? I've signed his wretched contract. I wanted to wait for a better offer but Madame insisted. Such a lot of money for a beginner, she said. So I gave in to her and I signed. So?

SALVATORE: But it's the *other* contract they are fighting about. Mathilde has been playing one off against the other. [*Distant shouting*] He's brought the mafia to dinner! [*Crash of china.*]

MELBA: But that's quite different. Strakosch can have me later on — *after* the Brussels debut.

SALVATORE: He won't let you *sing!* He is sueing the management of the theatre — of the Monnaie! What can we do? He will be in here next. He has brought the carta da tresette! [*Cutting his throat with his hand.*] I must hide the knives! Oh Madame, it's all my fault. *I* let him in that day when he came and interrupted your lesson. He gave a little something for my trouble. And Mathilde is so economic, you see. [*Realising*] My God! We are about to die! Forgive me, I *beg* of you. [*He clasps her, then sniffs her hair. Accusing.*] You have washed your hair. She has forbidden it. Only tonic water and a fine tooth comb. What if you caught cold?

MELBA: French lice are addicted to tonic water.

SALVATORE: [*sniffing*] And you have bathed!

MELBA: A bowl of cold water's a bit hard to sit in.

SALVATORE: Next you'll be riding *horses*. Mathilde has declared it is bad for the vocal cords.

MELBA: No. In Paris it's only bad for the bank balance. Cheer up Monsieur. I've given up that sort of riding.

[*Renewed sounds of broking crockery.*]

SALVATORE: On your knees!

[*He drops to his.* MELBA *refuses.*]

Pray! That your wretched husband won't turn up at the theatre tonight. Did you send him the cheque Mathilde arranged? Holy Mother — will it be enough? Any *more* scenes and the management will cancel. What am I *saying?* There's Strakosch! May the Virgin protect us!

[*The accompanist hands* MELBA *a telegram.*]

SALVATORE: [*snatching it to read*] It's from Lapissida, the manager at the Monnaie, at the opera? 'Strakosch has dropped dead. I await you at the theatre.' God is with us! Gilda lives!

[MELBA, *at her Brussels debut of 1887, sings 'Caro Nome' from Verdi's* Rigoletto, *beginning as a nervous young debutante and is transformed gradually into the supremely confident great soprano.*]

Gualtier Maldé! — nome di lui si amato
Ti scolpisci nel core innamorato!
Caro nome che il mio cor
Festi primo palpitar,
Le delizie dell'amor
Mi dêi sempre rammentar!
Col pensier il mio desir
A te sempre volerà,
E fin l'ultimo sospir,
Caro nome, tuo sarà.

[*Gualtier Maldè — The name of him I
cherish,
A name engraved upon my heart!
Dear name that makes my heart
Tremble with delight,*

Briging back to me
Memories of my first love
At the thought of my desire
To you my heart goes out,
And until my final breath,
Dear name, it shall be yours.]

SCENE TWELVE

1892. At the opera. Louis-Philippe, Duc d'Orleans, eldest son of the Pretender to the French throne and therefore the heir and known as the PRINCE *is sitting by* MELBA *in a box at the opera. They are watching the stage. He is handsome, glamorous and young. Schooled in England, he has only a slight accent.*

MELBA: Your Highness.
PRINCE: Don't call me that.
MELBA: It's all that I'm allowed, Philippe.
PRINCE: And not that.
MELBA: Tipon, then. [*Hesitating.*] Are we going to quarrel?
PRINCE: I'm in pain. My apologies for —
MELBA: No. There is no need to —. It *has* to end. Better I leave you here at the opera, listening to my rival. Eames is in good voice. I'll slip out. You'll hardly notice —
PRINCE: My father had no *right.*
MELBA: Your father had *every* right. The opera singer and the Prince? A cliche. A Prince about to be named as the co- respondent in a divorce? A commoner challenging the heir to the throne to a duel?
PRINCE: A non-existent throne. A non-existent duel.
MELBA: Charlie only wants you to look a coward. He'll never *fight* you.
PRINCE: Oh? You think not? I feel as if I've been shot.
MELBA: You'll recover.
PRINCE: No. But I will — console myself.

MELBA: [*stiffly*] So will I.

PRINCE: [*desperate*] Go if you must. Go to America. Be a great success with their unspeakably vulgar millionaires. But in a year come back. People find new scandals. By then —. If we were discreet —

MELBA: *You* discreet? The Tsar certainly doesn't think it possible.

PRINCE: That turnip. You were a superb Juliette. *He* should have been shouting bravos and applauding you as wildly as I did.

MELBA: Protocol. Of all people — that *you* should forget protocol and anticipate his approval! He could have had you thrown into jail instead of ordering you out of St Petersburg, cousin or not. Worse — he could have cancelled the opera season.

PRINCE: Your career means more to you than I do?

MELBA: Of course. Doesn't yours?

PRINCE: I have no choice. I was born to mine.

MELBA: So was I. The difference is that you *are* and I *became*. It's a matter of achievement.

[*She rises to leave. He grasps her hand and draws her back.*]

PRINCE: Not yet.

MELBA: Your Highness — the English don't care for our kind of open scandal. My name has been passed over for the Windsor command performance this year. The royal displeasure can be felt at the *box-office* in a matter of hours. *Without* the social set — the titles that bring the hangers-on — the diamond horse-shoe at Covent Garden would soon be only empty plush. And *I'd* be bankrupt. It's not a matter of snobbery. The price of being the Assoluta is high. I intend to pay it.

PRINCE: Am I to be sold off to meet your debts?

MELBA: Yes. [*Softening*] Oh my dear, there's no future for us. Can you see me in ten years time, trailing round after you and the very suitable wife they'll find for you? No decent woman would be able to receive me and no management would dare to employ me. Your family — on either side of the Channel — would see to that.

PRINCE: I have suggested a morganatic marriage to my
father.

MELBA: You've *what?*

PRINCE: He was appalled too.

MELBA: I should *think* so.

PRINCE: [*handing her a press clipping*] The press is saying
you are pregnant — that's *why* I — Is it true?

[MELBA *jerks away, refusing to answer.*]

PRINCE: Very well then. You leave me no alternative. I
will disturb you no further.

[*He rises, bows without looking at her, and exits.*]

MELBA: [*picking up the clipping which has fallen between
them and reading*] 'L'Evenement, the first of November
1891. Divorce papers have been served on Madame
Melba as opera fans and journalists crowded round the
door of her house today. She was extremely affected
by it, so much so, that for an hour she was prostrated
with a violent attack of nerves, followed by a session
of crying . . . The action today is, they say, provoked
by the particularly interesting situation of Madame
Melba. It is this that has determined Monsieur
Armstrong to break his silence. [*She slowly tears up
the clipping*]

[MELBA TWO *reads from a second clipping which she
shows to* MELBA *who takes it and also reads.*]

MELBA TWO: Thirty years after their liaison ended a certain
royal personage and a certain lady of the stage dined
together last night at the Ritz.

MELBA: There was no sign of the scars both must bear.

MELBA TWO: He from the failure of a subsequently
arranged marriage, . . .

MELBA:. . . the lack of an heir, . . .

MELBA TWO:. . . and the toll taken by a life led as an
explorer in exile from his native land, . . .

MELBA:. . . she from divorce and the loss of her only
child . . .

TOGETHER:. . . after she was declared an unfit mother.

MELBA: [*reading from a letter*] 'Hotel Ritz, Piccadilly, the
twenty-fifth of March, 1919. My dear Nellie, what can
I tell you of the tender emotion that I have felt again

after so many years? It seemed to me that it was
yesterday that I said au revoir to you and that I found
myself near to you the same, in spite of the age I then
had nearly thirty years ago. I was so happy to find
you in spite of your sufferings, moral and physical, the
same Nellie who has never changed and who remains
in my life,

MELBA TWO: sometimes so sad, the only constant and
faithful friend towards whom — even in the delirium
of death that I so closely escaped — my soul and heart
reached across space. For you know me and understand
me! In spite of all the world has done to separate one
from the other. I am satisfied because the confidence
you gave me is my recompense. Thank you for the
few moments in which you have really made me happy
in evoking the past years of my youth that I have relived
through you and with you. I count the minutes that
separate me from the moment when I will see you
tomorrow evening. I hope for longer than this evening?
I have so many things to say to you that I cannot write.
But that tomorrow will come of themselves from my
lips when I am near to you. I hope you will give me
time to tell you all that I have in my heart. Meantime,
my dear Nellie, I kiss most affectionately your pretty
hands and am always

MELBA: your old Tipon.'

[MELBA *who has slowly moved to the piano, sings
Chausson's 'Le temps des Lilas'.*]

Le temps des lilas et le temps des roses
Ne reviendra plus à ce printemps-ci;
Le temps des lilas et le temps des roses
Est passé, le temps des oeillets aussi.
Le vent a changé, les cieux sont moroses,
Et nous n'irons plus courir, et cueillir
Les lilas en fleur et les belles roses;
Le printemps est triste et ne fleurir.
Oh joyeux et doux printemps de l'année,
Qui vins l'an passé, nous ensoleiller,
Notre fleur d'amour est si bien fanée,

Las! Que ton baiser ne peut l'éveiller!
Et toi, que fais-tu? pas de fleurs écloses,
Point de gai soleil ni d'ombrages frais;
Le temps des lilas et le temps des roses
Avec notre amour est mort a jamais.

[*The time of lilacs and the time of roses*
Will not return again this spring;
The time of lilacs and the time of roses
Has gone, the time of carnations too.
The wind has changed, the skies are gloomy,
And we shall hurry no more to gather
The lilacs in bloom and the beautiful roses;
The spring is sad and will not come to
flower.
Oh, sweet and joyful season of the year,
Which last year came to bathe us in its sun-
light;
Our flower of love has withered so
Alas! Your kiss cannot revive it!
And you, what do you do? No more bud-
ding flowers,
No more bright sunshine or cooling shade;
The time of lilacs and the time of roses,
With our love, is forever dead.]

SCENE THIRTEEN

Sounds of children playing. MELBA *plays a child's game with the doll George who comes on with* MELBA TWO *who is carrying a bag as if about to go on a journey.*

MELBA:

Georgie, porgie, pudding and pie,
Mama kissed the boys and made them cry.
When your Mama came out to play
Your Father chased them all away.

Goodbye George. We'll have the holidays together. Daddy promised.

[MELBA *sings 'Comin' Through The Rye' to the doll, reluctant to let go.* MELBA TWO *begins to exit with the doll and the bag, but a phone rings as she is about to leave.* MELBA TWO *opens the bag and hands the phone to* MELBA, *then exits with the doll and the bag.*]

Gin a body meet a body, comin'through the rye,
Gin a body kiss a body, need a body cry?
Ilka lassie has her laddie,
Nane, they say, h'ae I!
Yet a' the lads they smile at me,
When comin' through the rye.

[*Answering the phone and listening*] To America! Can he do this? Legally? [*Listens.*] *This* mother's consent may *not* be required by the law, but surely it was common decency to let me know *before* Mr Armstrong could spirit the child out of the country. It *is* possible that I could have prevented it! Legally. It *is* possible I might have *wanted* to. It *is* possible that I'm not the monster you've been led to believe I am. And it is possible that I'll move heaven and earth to find my son.

[*She slams down the receiver. The sounds of children fade. She dials. Mechanical sound effects — crackling, under ocean cables, blurred voices, continue at each call after the first.*]

Operator? Get me the police.

[*As she dials each time she turns until she completes a circle.*]

Operator? Get me New York.

[*Gradually becoming frantic.*]

Operator? Get me Washington. Operator? Get me — Operator? There's only crackling sounds on the line. Operator? There's no answer. Get me — Operator? ... Operator?

[*Voiceover of operator with American accent.*]

V/O: Criterion Theatre, Boston? Call for Madame Melba from George Armstrong. Will you accept charges? I'm connecting you now.

MELBA: George? But your voice — yes, I suppose I should have expected it at eighteen, but —. The *advertisements* — is that how you found me! Tonight then after the concert. [*Listens*] Why do you *think* I took on all these backwoods tours? I kept hoping for clues — *some* trace of you. But I never expected you to come looking for *me*. I'll make it up to you. And — George, don't believe *all* they say. I had to earn a living. And what sort of life would it have been for you? You'd have been a hothouse plant. Charlie wanted hard work and horses for you and no women. Is that what you got? Was he right? [*Listens*] No! Don't bring champagne. I hate the stuff.

[*She sings a brief 'snatch' from 'Libiamo ne lieti calici' from Verdi's* La Traviata. *Overjoyed, she accepts champagne from the actor and there are toasts all round. She makes a face over the champagne but raises the glass.*]

Libiamo ne' lieti calici
che la bellezza infiora,
e la fuggevol ora
s'inebri a voluttà!
Libiam ne' dolci fremiti
che suscita l'amore,
poichè quell'occhio al core
onnipotente va!
Libiamo, amor fra i calici
più caldi baci avrà!

Tra voi saprò dividere
il tempo mio giocondo;
tutto è follia nel mondo ciò
che non è piacer!
Godiam, fugace e rapido
è il gaudio dell'amore,
è' un fior che nasce e muore,

nè più si puo goder!
Godiam, c'invita un fervido
accento lusinghier, ah! ah!

[Let's drink from the cup of joy
Here where beauty flourishes.
Let this fleeting moment be given over
To intoxicating pleasure.
Let's drink to the sweet stirrings
And tremors of love —
Then to eyes that pierce
To my very heart.
Let's drink from the cup of love
And to the wine that warms our kisses.

With you, my friends,
I shall laughingly pass my time.
The world is nought but folly,
And I'll have none of that.

Then live for joy, the joy of love,
Fleeting though it is;
For love is a flower
Which buds, then dies,
No more to be savoured.
So yield to its allure,
And enjoy every pleasure to the full!]

[MELBA *exits with a 'snatch' from 'Libiamo ne' lieti calici from Verdi's 'La Traviata'. The melody is taken up in a cracked voice by* SALVATORE, *who enters with a bottle of champagne and 2 glasses, one of which he is still filling from the bottle. He has newspapers under his arm. He is obviously trying to catch up with the disappearing* MELBA *to celebrate, but can't locate her. He searches as he sings, but gives up, parking the bottle and the glasses on the piano, invites the pianist to drink and pours a glass for him. As he downs his own glass he unfolds the paper as if expecting to read a flattering review of*

MELBA. *Realising that there is an item, then others,
that tell of her being about to attempt the role of
Brunnhilde, he becomes agitated and calls:*]

SALVATORE: Mathilde! Mathilde!

[*She enters. He thrusts the papers at her.*]

You must stop her. At once!

[MATHILDE *shakes out the paper, looking at him with
distrust.*]

MARCHESI: Melba? *That* is not possible.

SALVATORE: But she will ruin you — *us*!

MARCHESI: *That* is possible.

SALVATORE: She will be cutting her own throat. *Then*
who will come to the Marchesi for lessons? Who would
trust a *career* to us? She has come to see you. You
must —

MARCHESI: Yes, my dear. I *must*. We will drink on it.

[*They drink.* SALVATORE *exits in a hurry, bearing
away the bottle and glasses before he is obliged to
confront* MELBA *as she enters.*]

SCENE FOURTEEN

MARCHESI: I want a word with you. [*Brandishing
newspapers.*] Have you seen this? And this?

MELBA: There's always something. What is it this time?
Obscene acts with the stage hands? Poisoning off some
rival? Another Prince? You got what you wanted there
you can't have everything. Oh don't look so sour,
Madame. It's all publicity, isn't it?

MARCHESI: They say —

MELBA: They say? What say they? Let them say!

MARCHESI: [*tapping the paper*] You will *not* sing
Brunnhilde. Over my dead body!

MELBA: Where's the phone? I must order a wreath.

MARCHESI: You *can't* sing it.

MELBA: *I* will decide what *I* can sing, thank you. I'm
not Trilby and you're no Svengali. Not any more.

MARCHESI: I was right about the Prince. You got over it. You sang all the better. *Now* there many Princes but only one Melba. *Not* Svengali? Who sent you to Gounod?

MELBA: He's falling out of fashion.

MARCHESI: Are you afraid *you* are falling out of fashion?

MELBA: Bel canto opera is falling out of fashion. *I am* bel canto opera. But Wagner —

MARCHESI: You will turn gold into brass.

MELBA: I need a great composer.

MARCHESI: *You* chose Bemberg.

MELBA: Bemberg was a gelding — I forgot to look. I need a stallion in my stable.

MARCHESI: Puccini wrote *Butterfly* for you! Why don't you sing it?

MELBA: I can't remember the bloody orchestral cues.

MARCHESI: *You?* Huh! It is because you are no actress. I sent you to Bernhardt, but —

MELBA: Would they believe it was acting for me to play mother to a bastard?

MARCHESI: So! At last! You are learning what scandal can do to a career, eh? But the truth, now.

MELBA: It's that woman. The Met wants Nordica for Brunnhilde. I'll be damned if I let that upstart have it. Maybe — just maybe they want to replace me?

MARCHESI: Ah — you *are* afraid.

MELBA: Only fools think they're immortal.

MARCHESI: Then you will do this thing?

MELBA: I have to try it, Matilda.

MARCHESI: You will fail.

MELBA: *If* I fail at Brunnhilde I will *have* to find another way. Up. I refuse to fall . . . I'll go to Lucca. To Puccini. And I will learn *Boheme* from him. And one day, soon, I'll take that opera home. As I will take you home in everything I sing, everything I teach. I need to go back. Now, before —. I need to build. I need to know what they think of me. I need to — belong.

[MELBA *sings 'Donde lieta usci' from Puccini's* La Bohème.]

Donde lieta usci al tuo grido d'amore,
torna sola Mimi al solitario nido.
Ritorna un'altra volta
a intesser finti fior!
Addio, senza rancor.
Ascolta, ascolta. Le poche robe
aduna che lasciai sparse.
nel mio cassetto stan chiusi
quel cerchietto d'or,
e il libro di preghiere.
Involgi tutto quanto
in un grembiale e manderò il portiere.
Bada, sotto il guanciale
c'e la cuffietta rosa.
Se vuoi, se vuoi,
se vuoi serbarla a ricordo d'amor!
Addio, addio senza rancor.

[*From whence she came, gladly at the call
of love,
Mimi returns alone to her solitary haunt;
Returns once more to fashioning
Artificial flowers.
Farewell, without bitterness!
Listen, listen. The few small things
That I have left
Loose in my drawer
Are safely kept. The little gold chain
And the prayer book.
Wrap all of them in an apron
And I will call the porter.
But stay — beneath the pillow
There is a little pink bonnet.
If you wish, if you wish
Keep it as a memento of our love!
Farewell, farewell, without bitterness.*]

[*Applause and bravos at the end of the* Bohème *extract. All do a rapid-fire vaudeville comic-turn with music under as they circle.*]

SCENE FIFTEEN

MELBA TWO: On your guard! *This* role belongs to you — don't let Eames or Calve pinch it.

MELBA: The only thing of mine anyone has ever pinched is my — cheek.

MAN: [*as Caruso*] The fee for the Great Caruso is four hundred pounds! Not a penny less!

MELBA: And *my* fee is a pound more than Caruso, no matter what *he* gets.

MELBA TWO: Worth designs for you, doesn't he? Does he design for Tetrazzini?

MELBA: Tetrazzini? *Her* costumes were designed by Barnum and Bailey.

MELBA TWO: I love basses.

MAN: I adore baritones.

MELBA: I'd do anything for a tenor.

MAN: You know Madame Austral of course.

MELBA: Austral? Who's Austral?

MAN: But you sang in Aida with her last night!

MELBA: Oh — she was black, then.

MELBA TWO: Adelina Patti is dead!

MELBA: How could you tell?

MELBA TWO: And of course you know that Madame Selma Kurz has died.

MELBA: A good career move.

MELBA & MELBA TWO: Did you hear about the tenor who was so dumb the other tenors noticed?

MAN: Welcome to the Savoy Hotel, Madame Melba. [*Searching for keys*] Room — no, a suite. Would you like the Bridal?

MELBA: Heavens no. I'll just hang onto his neck until I drop off.

MELBA TWO: That girl has a truly lovely voice. She'll make a wonderful Juliette next season at the Garden.

MELBA: Not on your life. She's going to be out of season. I've got her a tour — to Iceland.

MAN: Madame Melba, won't you give us *one* little song?

MELBA: Certainly. If you give me *one* little cheque.

MELBA TWO: Did you hear that Tetrazzini is performing at the Hippodrome with dogs.

MELBA: [*giggles, then abruptly serious*] No comment. [*To the MAN*] Monsieur Escoffier do you have frog's legs?

MAN: But of course, Madame.

MELBA: Then hop into the kitchen and make me a sandwich.

MELBA TWO: Your rival — Nordica. She's getting married.

MAN: Has she told the groom about the men in her life?

MELBA TWO: She *said* — 'I've told him *everything*. I have nothing to conceal.'

MAN: What courage!

MELBA: What a *memory*.

MELBA TWO: Have you got A flat?

MELBA: Any key will do. I'll let myself in.

MAN: May I help you Madame?

MELBA: Deliver these.

MAN: At your convenience, Madame.

MELBA: Dear me, please — no! Is *nothing* private?

MELBA TWO: I do enjoy having Melba to stay: she makes you feel so at home in your own house.

MAN: Melba — an actress? One arm up — great emotion. Two arms up — passion.

MELBA TWO: What a bitch Galli-Curci is.

MELBA: No dear — *that's* a dog.

[*The MAN as CARUSO presses up against her.*]

CARUSO: Your tiny hand is frozen, let me warm it into life.

MELBA: I'd rather have a hot sausage, thanks.

MELBA TWO: Did you really tell Clara Butt to sing the Australians muck?

MELBA: They're a very earthy people. Ah — Monsieur Escoffier? Are we having your Peche Melba?

MELBA TWO: With sour cream? [MELBA TWO *sings a scale*]

MELBA: [*over this and to the MAN*] Tell me, do you keep *many* cats in your hotel?

MELBA TWO: Are you *really* running for Parliament? [*Music stops.*] It's here in *Truth!*

MELBA: *Truth?* That's the *last* thing I'd call John Norton's rag!

[JOHN NORTON, *back turned, is lit. He turns to the audience. He is the muckraking editor of* Truth *and speaks with a broad Australian accent.*]

SCENE SIXTEEN

NORTON: Marvellous Melba. Mellifluous Melba. Supreme Singer. Crowned Cantatrice and Monarch of Matchless Music though you be, your private and public conduct during your short six months sojourn in Australasia makes it compulsory that you should be told the truth.

[*The* ACCOMPANIST *and* MELBA TWO *as The Oz Public are lit together in another spot. They lower the pages of* Truth *which they have been reading, held high in front of their faces*]

WOMAN: Gawd!

MAN: I don't *believe* it!

WOMAN: [*loving it*] She *never* —

MAN: Sick? [*Reading, unbelieving*] *Drunk?* Postponed till next *week?*

[*They read, raising the papers as before.*]

NORTON: Your breaches of faith with the Australian people are as much due to champagne as to *real* pain. Moet and Chandon have a lot of misery and chagrin to answer for, especially among prima donnas. [*Taking a nip from a hip flask furtively.*]

WOMAN: [*nudging the* MAN] Hey! I've got tickets, but. Reckon I ought to ask for me money back?

MAN: Well, I don't *know* . . .

[*They read again, raising the papers.*]

NORTON: Then there's the matter of your conduct towards
those who are in any way dependent upon you. You
tried to 'take down' your tour organiser. *He* had to
take you to court to make you pay up.

WOMAN: [*lowering her paper*] And poor Miss Gill, what
about *her?*

MAN: She's bound to sue.

NORTON: *And* there's your flute player — cursing and
swearing at *him* in the coarsest terms.

WOMAN: Here, where's me tickets. [*Finding them and
thrusting them on the MAN, who exits in a hurry*] Cash
'em in.

NORTON: And God *alone* knows who *that* was coming out
of your room at Menzies at *3am* on a *Sunday* morning.

WOMAN: Hey, half a tick Bill. I've changed me mind.
Let's see what the old girl's *really* like.

[*Exit* NORTON *and* MELBA TWO/WOMAN. *The
Accompanist leads* MELBA *on to sing, bitterly,
ironically,* Home Sweet Home.]

> Mid pleasures and palaces though we may
> roam,
> Be it ever so humble, there's no place like
> home;
> A charm from the skies seems to hallow us
> there,
> Which, seek thro' the world, is ne'er met
> with elsewhere.
> Home, home, sweet, sweet, home.
> There's no place like home,
> Oh, there's no place like home.

SCENE SEVENTEEN

Enter OSCAR HAMMERSTEIN, *an American-Jewish
entrepreneur. It is 1905. He is trying to persuade* MELBA
*to come to New York to open his Manhattan Opera House,
a rival to the Met.*

MELBA: No, Mr Hammerstein, I will not. And please don't smoke.

HAMMERSTEIN: Fifteen hundred. That's my last offer. [*Rolling an unlit cigar in his mouth*] And who's smoking?

MELBA: I am not for sale, Mr Hammerstein. This is not an auction. And if you are not smoking then you are threatening to do so.

HAMMERSTEIN: Two thousand. And you can sing what you like, as little as you like. Queen at the new Manhattan, that's you.

MELBA: That's not how I do business.

HAMMERSTEIN: The Metropolitan Opera never gives you a chance. Why do you let them dictate to you? *You?* And for so little. Three thousand. And I give up smoking.

MELBA: No one dictates to *me*, Mr Hammerstein. I am going to take a bath. Goodbye, Mr Hammerstein. There's an ashtray over there. [*She closes door and prepares to bathe.*]

HAMMERSTEIN: [*on his knees, thrusting banknotes under the door and looking through the keyhole, cigar getting in the way.*] One, two, three, four, five hundred [*He continues to count.*]

MELBA: [*picking them up and counting as they appear*] One, two, three, four. . . I can't accept this . . . five . . .

HAMMERSTEIN: How can I open a new opera house without your help? Don't you realise you're the *only* singer in the world who could *destroy* the Metropolitan? *And* all those arrivistes on the Board? They barely speak to you. They hate us emigrants. Melba from the convict colonies and Hammerstein the upstart Jew.

MELBA: [*reacting*] I will hand this over to Mr Rothschild's bank. He'll keep it for you till you come for it. I won't sing for *money*, Mr Hammerstein.

HAMMERSTEIN: Not for money? But there must be something —

MELBA: [*opening the door and taking the cigar from his mouth*] The only reason I'll sing for *you*, sir, is that you're like the boy who murdered both his parents and then pleaded with the judge for mercy on the grounds that he was an orphan. You call that chutzpah. I call it bloody cheek, Mr Hammerstein. *That's* what we have in common and *that's* why I'll sing for you, sir. [*She puts the cigar in her mouth and Hammerstein lights it. She takes one puff.*]

[*Flirting with him, she sings Thurlow Lieurance's Indian Love Song, 'By the Waters of Minnetonka', in English.*]

Moon Deer,
How near
Your soul divine.
Sun Deer,
No fear
In heart of mine.
Skies blue
O'er you,
Look down in love;
Waves bright
Give light
As they move.
Hear thou
My vow
To live, to die.
Moon Deer,
Thee near,
Beneath this sky.

[*L'oiseau des nuits,
Au vent s'enfuit,
Et l'eau des rives,
Plaintive fremit.
L'echo des bois,
Tout pleure en moi,
Me rappelle fidele,
Sa voix.
La lune,
aux cieux,*

N'avait d'attraits
Qu'en son reflet,
Dans ses doux yeux.
Dernier essor,
Supreme accord,
Le chant se brise,
La brise s'endort.
Le flot, sans bruit,
Passe et vers lui,
Seul encore J'implore l'oubli.]

SCENE EIGHTEEN

MELBA *and* MELBA TWO *talk. With war sounds and music under until 'up and at 'em.'*

MELBA TWO: The war is going to be quite fun after all.

MELBA: Concerts for the relief fund . . .

MELBA TWO: Belgian flags and gum leaves round the stage . . .

MELBA: Leading on a British Bulldog with a diamond studded leash . . .

MELBA TWO: Everyone cheering.

MELBA: Auctioning flags . . .

MELBA TWO: Singing *Rally Round the Banner*. . .

MELBA: My girls — I *must* have my girls sing next time.

MELBA TWO: Next time you take classes, line them up. Along the stairs, toes at the edge of the red carpet. What's your Conservatorium *for?*

MELBA: They must *all* learn *Over There* and *Tipperary* and *Australia Will Be There.*

MELBA TWO: If they can't obey rules of dress and conduct, how are they to learn the discipline of *singing?*

MELBA: They can come to Coombe next Sunday. I shall put on my chef's hat and apron and cook a chop picnic for them.

TOGETHER: It's a battle! 'Up and at 'em!'
[*Music underscoring ceases.*]

MELBA: Something's happening. Empty sleeves. Crutches. What's that place — Gallipoli? No-one wants to look.

MELBA TWO: *I'll* make them look. And pay for the privilege. These are *our* men and they'll starve if we don't help out.

MELBA: Everything's changing. The ship Home was uncomfortable. Lots of broken portholes, and so *dirty* from the war.

MELBA TWO: London is untidy. Haphazard.

MELBA: So gray and strange. Not the London I knew.

MELBA TWO: At least Covent Garden is still there.

MELBA: Making up my face backstage on opening night — I felt I was looking at a ghost.

MELBA TWO: So many new faces in the corridors.

MELBA: In other dressing room mirrors.

MELBA TWO: So many friends — gone.

MELBA: I sang to the dead.

MELBA TWO: There are no diamonds glittering back out of the half-dark now. No smell of women's bouquets.

MELBA: No roses on the royal box.

MELBA TWO: Only tweed coats and shabbiness in the stalls.

MELBA: My bright world has gone. Forever.

MELBA TWO: And I *resent* it!

[*They move to another place.*]

MELBA: I can't seem to stop travelling, in spite of my age. Am I looking for something, or is it boredom, do you think?

MELBA TWO: I keep losing my temper with people who don't deserve it.

MELBA: I've done everything I want to.

MELBA TWO: But I'm still — restless.

TOGETHER: I've got George. And I should be grateful but — . Mustn't be maudlin.

MELBA: The voice is going at the top. Like me.

MELBA TWO: But what's left is worth hearing, though it's mostly technique. Chappell's are publishing my *Method*. Nice royalties.

MELBA: Those old records of twenty years back. Tinny.

MELBA TWO: I'm recording again. There's this new electric system. I'll be among the first generation of singers to hand on their art intact this way.

MELBA: And I'll live on through my girls. That's my gift to the nation. And to Maestro Cecchi.

MELBA TWO: Maybe I'll never be known as the Mother of Australian Music — maybe the matriarch. But I gave other women a pride in my achievement.

MELBA: I showed 'em what we could do, didn't I?

[MELBA *sings in English* Songs my Mother Taught Me *by Anton Dvorak.* ACCOMPANIST *exits.*]

Songs my mother taught me
in the days long vanished;
seldom from her eyelids
were the teardrops banished.
Now I teach my children
each melodious measure;
oft the tears are flowing,
oft they flow from my memry's treasure

[*Als die alte Mutter
mich noch lehrte singen,
Thränen in den Wimpern
gar so oft ihr hingen.
Jetzt wo ich die Kleinen
sel ber üb' im Sange,
rie selt's in den Bart oft,
rie selt's oft von der braunen Wange!*]

[MELBA *comes downstage and sits alone.* BEVERLY NICHOLLS *the ghost-writer of the memoirs and a handsome young English man-about-town, brings her a shawl and puts it round her.*]

SCENE NINETEEN

MELBA: I'm very fond of you Bev. You mustn't take this to heart. We've almost finished the book anyway.

BEV: I don't *like* this gigolo image.

MELBA: I *do* pay for your services. As a writer.

BEV: Are we having one of our furies? Have a care it might wind up in the memoirs. Be a nice gutsy change from all that whitewash.

MELBA: It *has* to be a whitewash job. It's twenty years since Norton but I'm still living it down. The others have all done it. Anyway I *want* to be remembered. And I'll do *anything* to see I am.

BEV: I'd *like* to write about 'the great singer', the performer, ageing — the destruction of the voice, the art. About the clinging to life, the using of it. The *urge* — for a woman — to leave something.

MELBA: Oh go and write your wretched novel. Make your *heroine* as ugly as you like. They'll say it's me, but I don't give a damn. You want to be top dog? So grow teeth and learn how to use 'em. Use *me*.

BEV: You'll let me stay then?

MELBA: Certainly not. It's a tough old world, lov, as you're about to find out.

[MELBA *sings* Believe Me If All Those Endearing Young Charms; MELBA *at piano*.]

Believe me, if all those endearing young charms
Which I gaze on so fondly today,
Were to change by tomorrow,
And fleet in my arms,
Like fairy gifts fading away,
Thou wouldst still be ador'd
As this moment thou art,
Let thy loveliness fade as it will,
And around the dear ruin each wish of my heart,
Would entwine itself verdantly still.

It is not while beauty and youth are thine
own
And thy cheeks unprofan'd by a tear,
That the fervour and faith of a soul can be
known,
To which time will but make thee more
dear;
No, the heart that has truly loved never for-
gets,
But as truly loves on to the close,
As the sun flower turns on her god when
he sets,
The same look that she gave when he rose.

[MELBA TWO *enters with a glassless mirror frame*]

SCENE TWENTY

MELBA TWO: What do you think? A bit off the nose or just the chin? Wonder how long before the bruises go? I can't *wait*.

MELBA: A facelift. Vain old biddy!

MELBA TWO: Wait till a few old flames get relit.

MELBA: It's new. It's dangerous.

MELBA TWO: So bring me flowers if it's to be opening night in the other place. I *like* to look my best. Come on. Let's go and do it. Now!

MELBA: I can't.

MELBA TWO: You promised you'd . . .

MELBA: . . . I'd go. When the time came. I'd. .;

MELBA TWO: . . . You'd go. Gracefully. Well?

MELBA: Just once more. An encore?

MELBA TWO: No! A *little* dignity.

MELBA: Please! If I don't sing I'll die.

MELBA TWO: Rubbish! Women like you never *die*.

MELBA: No one but *no* one is *like* me.

MELBA TWO: No. I'll give you that much.

MELBA: I'll go — if I *must*. But on *my* terms.
[*Recorded applause.* MELBA *sings in English
Francesco Tosti's* Goodbye.]

Falling leaf and fading tree,
Lines of white in a sullen sea,
Shadows rising on you and me.
Shadows rising on you and me.
The swallows are making ready to fly,
Wheeling out of a windy sky,
Goodbye summer, goodbye, goodbye!

Hush, a voice from the far away!
'Listen and learn' it seems to say,
'All the tomorrows shall be as today.'
'All the tomorrows shall be as today.'
The cord is frayed, the cruse is dry,
The link must break and the lamp must die.
Goodbye to hope, goodbye, goodbye!

What are we waiting for, oh my heart?
Kiss me straight on the brows and part
Again, again, my heart, my heart.
What are we waiting for, you and I?
A pleading look, a stifled cry,
Goodbye forever, goodbye, goodbye!

[*Cadon stanche le foglie al suol,
Bianche strisce serpon sull'onda,
Lieve nebbia nell'aria fonda,
Sembran freddi i rai del sol.
Le rondinelle la sciano il nido
Verso altro lido, Le trae desio:
Estate, addio! Addio, estate,
addio,addio!*

*Una voce lontan lontan,
'Odi e impara' sembra gridare,
'Non diverso dal l'oggi è il doman,'
'Gioia e duolo, polve ed altare.'*

Ogni legame mortal si spezza,
Copre l'oblio Fielee dolcezza.
O speme, addio, addio! O speme, addio,
addio!

Perché aspettar tuttor, Oh! dolce amor?
Un sol bacio mi dà,
Poscia ten va. Un altro ancor, un altro
ancor.
un altro ancor. Pegno d'eterna fe da te
voglio,
Perchè il tuo cor è fatalmente mio
Per sempre addio, per sempre, addio, addio!
Per sempre addio!]

[*Applause. The original recorded speech comes up*
and takes over from MELBA *as lights dim while she*
stands there, staring.]

MELBA: [*with recording*] And now there's only one more
word to say, and that is farewell. I won't say goodbye
because farewell is such a beautiful word. I am sure
you all know that it's part of a prayer and means
'fare-thee-well', which I wish you all and I feel sure
that you wish me the same.

[*Applause.*]

THE END